A Child of God Dies...
from one grieving heart to another

Evangelist Rod Black

About the Cover

Daisies were my sweetheart's favorite flower. Not only do the flowers remind me of her, but of the beautiful life we shared together.

After the love of my life left for Heaven, in the midst of my grief was a hint of anticipation. God had been so good to me up until now; what would the future hold? I realized that I had come to the close of an amazing chapter of my life, and that my Father above was picking up the pen to begin a brand new chapter! The sunrise signifies hope within, as I look forward to what God has in store for me.

The soft touch is to acknowledge the tenderness of my Heavenly Father, as He has been leading me into the first few pages in this new chapter of my life.

When a Child of God Dies...

from one grieving heart to another

Evangelist Rod Black

Sermon & Song Ministries

Copyright 2021 Roderick Earl Black, Jr. All rights reserved.

No part of this book may be used, copied, or reproduced in any way without prior written permission from the copyright holder.

All Scripture quotations are from the King James Bible.

Just Beyond My Reach ©Debra I. Black
I Have Just Begun to Live ©Debra I. Black

ISBN 978-1-7379077-0-1

Available at a discount for bulk purchase.

Printed and bound in the USA by:
Bible and Literature Missionary Foundation
Shelbyville, Tennessee

Sermon and Song Ministries
P.O. Box 109
Ravenna, Ohio 44266
sermonandsong.org
330-472-3540
sermonandsong@gmail.com

Table of Contents:

Foreword   7

Introduction   9

Part One
Events That Take Place
When a Child of God Dies   17

CHAPTER 1
He Sees the Glory of God   19

CHAPTER 2
The Silver Cord is Loosed   23

CHAPTER 3
He is Carried by Angels   27

CHAPTER 4
To be Absent from the Body is to be
Present with the Lord   29

Part Two
How You and I Should React When the Lord
Takes Our Loved One Home   33

CHAPTER 5
Lessons From Job   35

CHAPTER 6
David Worshipped God, Then Broke His Fast 41

CHAPTER 7
Ezekiel Continued Serving God 45

CHAPTER 8
God Offers Comfort to the Mourner 49

CHAPTER 9
Verify Your Reservation for Heaven 55

A Song from Debbie 60

Music by Debbie Black 62

Debbie Black Memorial
Church Pianist Scholarship Fund 63

An Additional Resource 64

Foreword

*G*rief is natural emotion when a loved one dies; it is also a healing process. There is an emptiness that comes with death that desires comfort and answers. The Psalmist referred to death as the "valley of the shadow." It is a dark place with a loneliness that cannot be explained, only experienced. The death of a loved one also brings confusion and questions for those who are left to grieve.

Evangelist Rod Black writes from a heart of experience. From a compassionate heart, he shares Scripture that unravels the confusion and answers the difficult questions that accompany the death of a loved one. This book will comfort and guide the grieving soul through the healing process of grief.

Evangelist Rod Black glorifies God and honors Debbie's life and memory in sharing his heart in *When a Child of God Dies*.

Dr. Don Woodard, Pastor
Beacon Baptist Church
Salem, VA

Rod and Debbie Black

Introduction:

On February 18, 2021, my wife of 38 ½ years went home to be with the Lord. For just over two years, Debbie had battled Glioblastoma Multiforme (GBM), an extremely aggressive form of brain cancer. Although, through the years she had suffered with other physical ailments as well, you rarely heard her complain. She often commented about how she loved life.

Debbie and I were both raised in Christian homes and saved as children. Going to church and trying our best to live for the Lord was all we knew. We had each surrendered our lives to serve God and were enrolled in different Bible colleges when we met. Our churches had gone together to rent a bowling alley in Alliance, Ohio for an all-night activity, following our respective watch night services December 31, 1980. It was about 2:00 in the morning that New Year's Day that a mutual friend, Bro. Monte Watts, introduced us to each other. Debbie and I were married June 19, 1982. We served the Lord together in various ministries. The first was in southern Ohio where I was an associate pastor. Later, we planted a church in Northwest Pennsylvania and were there a few years. Next, we moved to the Thumb of Michigan where I pastored a small church. Then, we found ourselves back in our home area where we actively served the Lord in church until He led us to go into evangelism in the spring of 2002. It was then that Sermon and Song Ministries was born. During these many years, Debbie taught in three different Christian schools and home schooled our four children. All the while she continued composing music for the Lord, which, by the way, she actually started doing while she was still a teenager. Our best guess would be that she probably wrote well over 200 songs.

Debbie was very involved in Sermon and Song Ministries. Not only did she sing and write music, but she was my secretary and traveled by my side most of the time. In fact, she was with me on a ministry trip in Florida when she was diagnosed with the cancer. She loved to speak for mother daughter banquets and other ladies' meetings. In the churches we had the opportunity to minister in, Debbie was an encouragement to many pastors' wives and other ladies. Debbie's greatest desire was to make a difference in the lives of others. Most who knew her would say that she definitely accomplished that goal. However, she still left behind many unfulfilled dreams; there was so much more that she wanted to do. It is hard for us to understand why so often we cannot seem to fulfill all of our dreams, especially when they are God—honoring ambitions. Although this troubled Debbie at times, she seemed to be at peace with whatever the Lord would allow her to accomplish. I had forgotten about a poem she had written many years ago but found it in the file cabinet

> *Debbie's greatest desire was to make a difference in the lives of others.*

while looking through her *lyrics and song ideas* file. As I read the poem, I cried the whole way through. It helped me to accept God's decision to take my wife home even though she had so much more to offer. I would like to include it in hopes that it will be a help to you as it was to me.

Just Beyond My Reach

There have been so many things
I thought I'd like to do—
Noble, sweet ambitions,
And soon my musings grew;
They blossomed into lovely dreams
Of actions, song, and speech;
But my heart was disappointed—
They were just beyond my reach.

In the garden of my dreams
Are flow'rs of ev'ry hue;
So fragrant and alluring,
But are they right and true?
Please come into my garden, Lord,
And pull each selfish bloom,
That I might have the best of dreams—
A dream that's straight from You!

There is One Who knows me well,
Yet loved me from the start;

He is the Rose of Sharon,
Who lives within my heart!
And when I'm disappointed
Over lofty dream for me,
I'll think about my Saviour,
Whose dream was Calvary.

So if there is some flow'ry dream's
Fulfillment I don't see,
I'll trust my Heav'nly Father
To know what's best for me.
And when I see my Saviour's face
And worship at His feet,
I'll never have another dream
That is just beyond my reach.

Just beyond my reach?
I could not understand
Why the Lord prevented
What seemed the best of plans;
I gaze into my empty hands
And fall upon my knees;
And in that time of stillness,
My Father speaks to me.
There were reasons that those dreams of mine—
Such lovely plans within my mind—
Were plucked because of loving grace
And by Wiser Hands moved to a place
That was just beyond my reach.

Debbie was only 62 years old when she left for Heaven. She and I, along with hundreds of Christian friends, had been, in faith, asking God for healing. I am sure that God heard our prayers; however, in His infinite wisdom, He chose to take His precious daughter home to be with Him. We did our best to honor her memory with a first-class homegoing celebration. The congregation sang a few hymns and several of the songs that Debbie had written were featured as well. Each of our children had several nice things to say about their mom. Our pastor, Dr. David W. Ballert, did an outstanding job reflecting on her life and preaching a gospel message. The whole service lasted about 2 ½ hours! We played Debbie's piano CD, *Songs of God's Wonderful Peace,* during the calling hours. A large crowd attended, and many watched by way of livestream. In addition, an unbelievable number of folks have since taken the time to view the service on either YouTube or Facebook. Many have commented that it was one of the most uplifting funeral services they had ever seen.

We had a celebration, and I could not have been more pleased with the service; however, it was hard for me to say goodbye to my sweetheart. *I knew that her suffering was over, she is in a better place, I will see her again;* you know, all the things people say to try to comfort you. I also knew that I was going to miss her tremendously—I was right.

The next day I asked the Lord, "What do you want me to preach tomorrow morning?" The message He gave me that Saturday is the foundation for this book. Looking back, I think my sermon that Sunday morning was more for me than anyone else. I have since preached it in several churches, many have said that it helped them. Some changes have been made and several thoughts and Scripture references have been added. The basic message is the same. This is a topic that hits close to home more often than we would like. In fact, only two weeks after Debbie passed away, my mom, Betty Black, also left for her eternal home in Heaven. I miss them greatly. I am so thankful that they both knew Jesus Christ as their personal Saviour and that I will see them again.

My prayer is that the following thoughts from God's Word will be a help and comfort to you.

The Apostle Paul said in Philippians 1:21, "For to me to live is Christ, and to die is gain." Paul did not fear death but rather, from his writings, we conclude that he may have actually looked forward to it. For the Christian, death is merely the passageway to the blessed hope of eternal life in glory. David said in Psalm 23:4, "Yea, though I walk through the valley of the shadow of death, I will fear no evil: for thou art with me; thy rod and thy staff they comfort me." If you and I could somehow view death through the eyes of the departed Christian, I expect that our fears would diminish greatly. I really believe that from the departing saint's perspective, death is a wonderful experience. We see our

> *Imagine how much our Heavenly Father looks forward to His children coming home!*

Heavenly Father's perspective on death in Psalm 116:15, "Precious in the sight of the LORD is the death of his saints." Debbie and I so looked forward to our adult children coming home for a visit. They had obviously been in our home before, and of course they would have to leave again. On the other hand, God's children have never seen the splendor of Heaven or the mansion that He prepared for them... and they will never have to leave! Imagine how much our Heavenly Father looks forward to His children coming home! Friend, do not begrudge God of someone who is precious in His sight.

Several folks have said, "It seems like God takes the best ones." I don't know—perhaps He does. I had this thought: He probably loves her even more than I do! In reality, she was His before she was ever mine. Debbie was a special gift from God for which I will be forever grateful.

Many people are unaware of what actually transpires upon the death of a Christian. According to the Word of God, there are several events that take place when a child of God Dies. We will detail four of these in the first section. In the last half of the book, we will address what the Scriptures have to say about how you and I should react when the Lord takes our loved one home.

Part One

*Events That Take Place
When a Child of God Dies*

CHAPTER 1

He Sees the Glory of God

The first thing I want to bring to your attention is that according to Acts 7:54-60, when a child of God dies, he sees the glory of God.

> "When they heard these things, they were cut to the heart, and they gnashed on him with their teeth.
>
> But he, being full of the Holy Ghost, looked up stedfastly into heaven, and saw the glory of God, and Jesus standing on the right hand of God,
>
> And said, Behold, I see the heavens opened, and the Son of man standing on the right hand of God.
>
> Then they cried out with a loud voice, and stopped their ears, and ran upon him with one accord,
>
> And cast him out of the city, and stoned him: and the witnesses laid down their clothes at a young man's feet, whose name was Saul.
>
> And they stoned Stephen, calling upon God, and saying, Lord Jesus, receive my spirit.
>
> And he kneeled down, and cried with a loud voice, Lord, lay not this sin to their charge. And when he had said this, he fell asleep." (Acts 7:54-60)

According to Scripture, we know that Jesus is normally seated at the right hand of the Father. In verse 56 it appears that Jesus actually gave Stephen, the first Christian martyr, a standing ovation! (Stephen may have been the only Christian to receive this honor.) In addition, verse 55 tells us that Stephen *"saw the glory of God."* I have no reason to believe that this particular experience was unique to Stephen.

In Exodus 33:18, Moses asked God if he could see His glory. God partially granted his request by giving him a limited view. I believe that when a child of God dies, he sees an uninhibited view of the glory of God! Many who have been with a dying saint at their time of passing have indicated that they must have seen something. Debbie had been asleep for two days; although she passed peacefully, I did not see any change in her expression. However, I have been told that it is not uncommon to see a look of contentment or even anticipation on the face of a Christian in their last moments of life. Some who had not moved for quite some time raised their arms toward Heaven, while others actually raised up in the bed with outstretched arms. One lady whose eyes had been closed for several days, opened them just before she died. Friend, I believe they saw the glory of God! Although I mentioned it earlier, I would like to again reference the often quoted 23rd Psalm. In verse 4, the Bible says:

> *The cold dark valley transforms into a threshold leading to the splendors of Heaven.*

> *"Yea, though I walk through the valley of the shadow of death, I will fear no evil: for thou art with me; thy rod and thy staff they comfort me."* (Psalm 23:4)

The God of all comfort walks with us through the valley of the shadow of death. This is a walk we have never taken before, to a place we have never been before; a place that would seem to be dark and scary. It is there that His rod and staff comfort us as He reveals His glory to a dying saint. The cold dark valley transforms into a threshold leading to the splendors of Heaven.

Although our study deals primarily with the death of God's children, I must mention that a lost man's death bed experience is quite different. Many unsaved people have had a horrified look on their face, some even screaming out in terror. I do not know what they see but apparently it is not a pleasant sight.

CHAPTER 2

The Silver Cord Is Loosed

S olomon tells us in Ecclesiastes 12:6-7 that when a child of God dies the silver cord is loosed.

> *"Or ever the silver cord be loosed, or the golden bowl be broken, or the pitcher be broken at the fountain, or the wheel broken at the cistern.*
>
> *Then shall the dust return to the earth as it was: and the spirit shall return unto God who gave it."* (Ecclesiastes 12:6,7)

The silver cord is only mentioned this one time in Scripture. It is difficult to establish the meaning of a phrase in the Bible with any degree of certainty when there do not seem to be any cross references with which to compare. In most cases I will compare Scripture with Scripture to discern the meaning of God's Word rather than run to commentaries to see what other fallible men may think. The King James Bible itself is by far the most accurate and complete Bible dictionary and commentary available. I love my King James Bible! That being said, at times I will compare my conclusions with those of some of the great Bible scholars of the past. In this case, the majority of the commentaries I read suggested that these four items listed in Ecclesiastes 12:6 referred to a physical application rather than a spiritual one. However, some concluded as I have that the silver cord is the spiritual connection between the body and soul of man. Although the silver cord is not mentioned in any other verse, a general understanding of God's Word regarding the body and soul of man leads me to this conclusion. Without a soul, the body is lifeless. After God created Adam's body, He breathed life into that lump of clay; only then did Adam become a living soul.

> *"And the L*ORD *God formed man of the dust of the ground and breathed into his nostrils the breath of life; and man became a living soul."* (Genesis 2:7)

Since you and I can only see our bodies but not our souls, our thought process is often backward. We tend to think only in the physical realm. You see, I am an immortal soul living in a mortal body. My body will die but my soul lives on. When a child of God, or anyone for that matter, departs for eternity, their body dies; the soul is separated from the body. The silver cord, I believe, is the connection between the body and soul. The silver cord would be somewhat like the umbilical cord that connects the baby to its mother. Once the cord is cut the baby cannot return to the mother's womb. Doctors have in extreme cases carefully removed a baby from its mother's womb without damaging the umbilical cord. Surgery was performed on either the baby or the mother, and the baby then placed back inside its cozy little home. Again, once the cord is cut the baby can never return to the womb. In similar fashion you may have heard someone tell of an *out of body experience*.

One man supposedly hovered over his body in an operating room and observed while doctors and nurses performed surgery. The Apostle Paul told of a man who may have had an out of body experience.

> *"I knew a man in Christ above fourteen years ago, (whether in the body, I cannot tell; or whether out of the body, I cannot tell: God knoweth;) such an one caught up to the third heaven.*
>
> *And I knew such a man, (whether in the body, or out of the body, I cannot tell: God knoweth;)*
>
> *How that he was caught up into paradise, and heard unspeakable words, which it is not lawful for a man to utter."* (II Corinthians 12:2-4)

I have also heard similar accounts from people in our time. I cannot tell you for sure if any of the stories you hear or read about are legit or not. I can tell you that when the silver cord is loosed, the soul will not return to the body until the time of the Rapture. The Bible tells us that when the trumpet sounds, the bodies of the saints which have died will be raised from the dead and will be transformed into incorruptible, immortal bodies. The body and soul will be reunited for eternity! (I Corinthians 15:52-54)

CHAPTER 3

He Is Carried by Angels

*T*hirdly we learn in Luke 16:22 that when a child of God dies, he is carried by angels.

> *"And it came to pass, that the beggar died, and was carried by the angels into Abraham's bosom: the rich man also died, and was buried;*
> *And in hell he lift up his eyes, being in torments, and seeth Abraham afar off, and Lazarus in his bosom."*
> (Luke 16:22,23)

In this passage of Scripture, Jesus tells us of two men who died. One was a rich man; the other was a beggar named Lazarus. (By the way, neither man's financial status had any bearing on his eternal destiny. That being said, many times wealthy folks do seem to have a harder time recognizing their need of a Saviour.) The point I want to make here is that at least two angels carry the child of God to Heaven.

For those who may not understand, I see a necessity to explain the difference between Abraham's bosom and Heaven. Prior to Jesus being crucified and subsequently applying His blood on the Mercy Seat in Heaven, there was no permanent atonement for sin available. Hebrews

10:4 "For it is not possible that the blood of bulls and of goats should take away sins." Man could not enter Heaven until his sin was under the blood of Christ. The Old Testament saints had faith that the coming Messiah, Jesus Christ, would one day pay for their sin with His own precious blood. After the atonement was made on Calvary and the blood was applied on the Mercy Seat, Jesus personally took the saints who were waiting in Abraham's Bosom (aka Paradise) to Heaven. Since Jesus has already paid for our sins, we no longer go to Paradise but directly to Heaven. Forgive me if later on I refer to Paradise as Heaven; I do so for simplicity. Now, back to the angels!

> *God's children are personally escorted by angels, right into the presence of God!*

Just as Lazarus would not have known how to get to Abraham's bosom, you and I would probably have a hard time finding Heaven on our own. No worries, the Lord sends at least two angels to escort the child of God to his eternal home! The Scripture says *angels*, plural—that is certainly more than one. He might send a dozen, but my guess is two. To me, that is so cool!! The child of God doesn't float aimlessly around in space hoping to find Heaven, but rather, he is personally escorted by angels right into the presence of God! Shortly before Debbie took her last breath, I told her that soon, the angels would be coming to take her to Jesus.

CHAPTER 4

To be Absent from The Body Is to be Present with The Lord

Next, I want you to know that according to the Word of God, to be absent from the body is to be present with the Lord. This is significant because we care for our loved ones while they are here with us; rest assured, when they leave this world, they are not alone.

> *"For we know that if our earthly house of this tabernacle were dissolved, we have a building of God, an house not made with hands, eternal in the heavens.*
>
> *For in this we groan, earnestly desiring to be clothed upon with our house which is from heaven:*
>
> *If so be that being clothed we shall not be found naked.*
>
> *For we that are in this tabernacle do groan, being burdened: not for that we would be unclothed, but clothed upon, that mortality might be swallowed up of life.*
>
> *Now he that hath wrought us for the selfsame thing is God, who also hath given unto us the earnest of the Spirit.*
>
> *Therefore we are always confident, knowing that, whilst we are at home in the body, we are absent from the Lord:*
>
> *(For we walk by faith, not by sight:)*

> *We are confident, I say, and willing rather to be absent from the body, and to be present with the Lord.*
>
> *Wherefore we labour, that, whether present or absent, we may be accepted of him.*
>
> *For we must all appear before the judgment seat of Christ; that every one may receive the things done in his body, according to that he hath done, whether it be good or bad."* (II Corinthians 5:1-10)

If you would, please read verses 6 and 8 one more time.

> *"Therefore we are always confident, knowing that, whilst we are at home in the body, we are absent from the Lord:*
>
> *Wherefore we labour, that, whether present or absent, we may be accepted of him."* (II Corinthians 5:6,8)

As you can see, the Bible tells us that while we are at home in our bodies, we are absent from the Lord, but when we are absent from our bodies, we are present with the Lord! When a child of God dies, his soul is immediately present with the Lord. (Actually, there may be a brief delay while the angels escort the soul to Heaven. Do not let this be a concern, as the angels can travel so fast that you probably could not measure the time anyway.) One thing to be assured of—there are no detours on the way to Heaven. Some will tell you that first, the soul must spend a considerable amount of time in a place called purgatory. They might even imply that there is no guarantee that the soul will ever make it to Heaven. The main problem with the doctrine of purgatory is that it has no foundation in Scripture. Not only does the word not exist anywhere in the pages of the Bible but the concept is not there either. If a child of

God were required to face hundreds of years in a purifying fire before he ever attained Heaven, he obviously would not see the glory of God in his departing moments. Think back with me to what we read in the Gospel of Luke chapter 16. Jesus told us that Lazarus was carried by the angels into Abraham's bosom; He also told us that the rich man immediately went to Hell. Neither of these two men went to purgatory. Another account to consider is that of the thief on the cross. Jesus told him, "To day shalt thou be with me in paradise." In addition, notice that after Jesus applied His blood on the mercy seat, He took all of God's children who were waiting in Paradise directly to Heaven, not to purgatory. As we saw in II Corinthians a few moments ago, to be absent from the body is to be present with the Lord.

Part Two

How You and I Should React When the Lord Takes Our Loved One Home

*I*n this section of our study, although I will try to be kind and understanding, my concern is that in some cases, I may appear to be judgmental or harsh. This is certainly not my intention. May I remind you that this sermon was written and preached by yours truly just days after my wife's funeral. As I am writing, I am grieving—a tissue box sits right beside me. Friend, the truths of God's Word do not change according to our circumstances or our feelings. Please allow the next several pages to minister to your heart and help you through this difficult time in your life.

CHAPTER 5

Lessons from Job

The book of Job is the record of a series of events in a godly man's life. God was so impressed with Job that He bragged about him to the Devil. Satan, the accuser of the brethren, promptly accused Job of living for God only because God had blessed him so much. He told the Lord, "Put forth thine hand now, and touch all that he hath, and he will curse thee to thy face." Knowing the integrity of this man, God gave Satan liberty in Job's life, excepting his health. Later on, God allowed Satan to afflict him physically as well.

Job passed both tests with flying colors. In the end, the Lord rewarded Job with exactly double what he had lost during his time of testing. Interestingly, to replace his children, God gave him seven more sons and three more daughters—the same number that had died. You see, Job had not really "lost" his first ten children; they would be waiting for him in Heaven. God had, in fact, doubled all of Job's possessions!

As you read on you may notice that I seem to contradict myself in this matter of "losing" a loved one. Technically it is not a loss as I have just explained. It gives me great comfort to know that I did not really lose my Debbie, but that she is waiting for me in our heavenly home. That being said, there is a large hole in my heart; an emptiness was created when she left. To the grieving person, there is a loss.

In the next three points I want to consider how Job reacted to the devastating news that his children had all died. Let me challenge you to pattern your reaction in this difficult time to that of this godly man.

1. *Job Mourned His Loss*

Although he was a godly man of great faith, the Bible tells us in Job chapter 1 that, just like you and me, Job mourned his loss.

> *"While he was yet speaking, there came also another, and said, Thy sons and thy daughters were eating and drinking wine in their eldest brother's house:*
>
> *And, behold, there came a great wind from the wilderness, and smote the four corners of the house, and it fell upon the young men, and they are dead; and I only am escaped alone to tell thee.*
>
> *Then Job arose, and rent his mantle, and shaved his head..."* (Job 1:18-20a)

The rending of one's garment or shaving their beard in Job's day was a sign of mourning. It is quite natural and fully expected that you and I would mourn when we experience the loss of a loved one. Our mourning is a visible way for us to express our grief. It is not necessary for us to attempt to hide our grief from others. To completely refrain from mourning might falsely convey to our family and friends an inward feeling of apathy over our loss. On the other hand, do not feel that if your head is not hanging low or you are not crying you will appear to be callous. The ability to be strong in the midst of grief is not a bad thing, but when the tears begin to flow it's okay.

2. *Job Worshipped His God*

As we read the remainder of verse 20 as well as the following verse, we see Job worshipping the Lord.

> "...*and fell down upon the ground, and worshipped,*
>
> *And said, Naked came I out of my mother's womb, and naked shall I return thither: the LORD gave, and the LORD hath taken away; blessed be the name of the LORD.*" (Job 1:20b-21)

The Almighty God is <u>always</u> worthy of our worship and praise. In a general sense, God has been very good to us—in more ways than we could possibly count! When I reflect on God's goodness to me, even in relationship to my loss, I am overwhelmed. To begin with, the fact that He would give such a wonderful lady to be my wife still amazes me. Trust me, I did not  deserve someone like her. We enjoyed 38 ½ years of serving our Lord side by side. Raising our four children, traveling in evangelism, singing, having fun—we did everything together! My Bible gives me confidence that Debbie and I will someday be together again. I am not the least bit worthy of all God's blessings in my life. Yes, even in sorrow, I have reason to praise His name!

3. *Job Never Blamed God*

Not only did Job worship God, but he never blamed God for his loss. Job did not become angry toward God, nor did he shake his fist toward Heaven or scream at God. Notice what the Bible says in verse 22:

> *"In all this Job sinned not, nor charged God foolishly."*
> (Job 1:22)

The verse begins with the words, "In all this." Up until now we have not focused on the events immediately preceding the death of Job's children. To better understand all that was going on in Job's life at the time, I would ask that you take a minute to read Job 1:14-17.

> *"And there came a messenger unto Job, and said, The oxen were plowing, and the asses feeding beside them:*
>
> *And the Sabeans fell upon them, and took them away; yea, they have slain the servants with the edge of the sword; and I only am escaped alone to tell thee.*
>
> *While he was yet speaking, there came also another, and said, The fire of God is fallen from heaven, and hath burned up the sheep, and the servants, and consumed them; and I only am escaped alone to tell thee.*

> *While he was yet speaking, there came also another, and said, The Chaldeans made out three bands, and fell upon the camels, and have carried them away, yea, and slain the servants with the edge of the sword; and I only am escaped alone to tell thee."* (Job 1:14-17)

The very next messenger brings Job the devastating news that his 10 children had all died. Then the Lord says, "In all this Job sinned not, nor charged God foolishly". How quickly we tend to accuse God of doing us wrong. Friend, He loves you beyond measure. Never would God send any type of trouble or sorrow into your life in a mean, hateful or vindictive manner. Also, remember that God makes no mistakes. If the Lord allows, or even causes, things that bring heartache to our lives, though we may not understand at the time, He is always good and right. Consider what the Bible says in Romans 8:28:

> *"And we know that all things work together for good to them that love God, to them who are the called according to his purpose."* (Romans 8:28)

God loves you beyond measure!

This is a verse that is often quoted when everything is going our way; let it also minister to your heart when you are struggling. I know that God's decision not to heal Debbie was the right decision even though it was not the one I wanted. I have honestly wondered if part of the reason the Lord may have taken my Debbie home when He did, was to trigger the writing of this book which He would later use as a tool to help others. Some things we may never know this side of Heaven. The song writer of old said, "We'll understand it better by and by."

Perhaps you have had feelings of anger toward God. You are not alone as this is a very common reaction. We are human, and like the Apostle Paul, we must battle with our flesh daily. Be assured that your anger toward God has not caused His love for you to diminish in the slightest amount. The anger or bitterness you harbor in your heart toward God does not hurt Him nearly as much as it will hurt you. Try to resolve your differences with God and ask His forgiveness. As in other areas of our lives, learn to trust Him, even when we may disagree. There are a few people in this world that I trust completely—I know they would never hurt me in any way. If I can trust a man, certainly I can trust my loving Heavenly Father. Please, my friend, follow Job's example and do not be angry with God. In a later chapter, we will look at the kindness of God, and how He comforts His children in times of grief.

CHAPTER 6

David Worshipped God, Then Broke His Fast

*I*n this chapter, we will examine the way King David handled losing his child in death. This is something that I have never personally experienced. If you have lost a child, my heart goes out to you. I cannot imagine the pain you must feel. It is always hard to say goodbye to a loved one, but in your case, you may not have even had the opportunity to get to know your child before he or she left for Heaven. Thank God for the promise of Heaven! Although I do not have a child there, I long for the day that I will meet my little brother and several unborn grandchildren who are waiting for me. David understood exactly what you are going through. In a general sense, each of these chapters applies to all of us, for we each have either experienced the death of a loved one or will someday.

In II Samuel 12:15-23, David, with confidence that he would see his child again, worshipped God then broke his fast.

> *"And Nathan departed unto his house. And the* LORD *struck the child that Uriah's wife bare unto David, and it was very sick.*

David therefore besought God for the child; and David fasted, and went in, and lay all night upon the earth.

And the elders of his house arose, and went to him, to raise him up from the earth: but he would not, neither did he eat bread with them.

And it came to pass on the seventh day, that the child died. And the servants of David feared to tell him that the child was dead: for they said, Behold, while the child was yet alive, we spake unto him, and he would not hearken unto our voice: how will he then vex himself, if we tell him that the child is dead?

But when David saw that his servants whispered, David perceived that the child was dead: therefore David said unto his servants, Is the child dead? And they said, He is dead.

Then David arose from the earth, and washed, and anointed himself, and changed his apparel, and came into the house of the L ORD, *and worshipped: then he came to his own house; and when he required, they set bread before him, and he did eat.*

Then said his servants unto him, What thing is this that thou hast done? thou didst fast and weep for the child, while it was alive; but when the child was dead, thou didst rise and eat bread.

And he said, While the child was yet alive, I fasted and wept: for I said, Who can tell whether G OD *will be gracious to me, that the child may live?*

But now he is dead, wherefore should I fast? can I bring him back again? I shall go to him, but he shall not return to me." (II Samuel 12:15-23)

Before I focus on the main thought for this chapter, I must draw your attention to a truth we learn from verse 23: **When babies die, they always go to Heaven.** David knew that no amount of prayers or fasting could bring that child back, the silver cord had been loosed. David knew that his baby was in Heaven. He also knew that he himself would someday go to Heaven (I am so glad we can know that!) and would see his child again. Children who are too young to recognize their sinful condition and their need for a Saviour go directly to Heaven when they die. Although according to the Bible, baptism has no saving power, some religions will tell you that only babies who are baptized go to Heaven. We know that David's child had not been baptized, as there was no water baptism in the Old Testament. God had given David confidence that he would see his precious little baby in Heaven someday.

> *David moved forward with his life.*

Please forgive the rabbit trail—back to the subject... Like Job, David also worshipped the Lord. He is always worthy of our worship, even when we are unhappy with our circumstance. We also read in verse 20 that after David worshipped, he sat down to a meal. Notice that even though he was no doubt grieving, David continued on with his life. It appears that he took a shower, splashed on a little cologne, put on some nice clothes, went to church, and then finished out the day with a fine meal. Friend, can I encourage you to follow David's example? Get out of the house and do your best carry on. David went to the house of the Lord. I can assure you that singing hymns with the congregation, hearing the choir lift their voice to Heaven, or listening to a soloist sing a special will bless your soul! Then the pastor stands up and proclaims the Word of God! Wow! During the invitation, a soul walks the aisle and gets saved! After the service is over, we stand around and fellowship with Christian friends! I absolutely love being in the house of God!!! Like David did, try to move forward with your life.

CHAPTER 7

Ezekiel Continued Serving God

This chapter deals with exactly what I went through. Ezekiel was a man of God whose wife had passed away. As I mentioned in the previous chapter, although the particulars will vary, each of these Bible examples can be applied in our own lives.

Ezekiel tells us that his wife died, and the very next day he continued serving the Lord.

> "So I spake unto the people in the morning: and at even my wife died; and I did in the morning as I was commanded." (Ezekiel 24:18)

Ezekiel took no time off for grieving—not even a few days. You see, he was a servant of the Most High God. The work of God was more important to Ezekiel than his feelings of sorrow. Please notice it is not that Ezekiel did not grieve, but that he did not stop serving God *while* he grieved. Not only is serving the Lord more important than any other activity, service for Him also brings more joy and satisfaction to our lives than anything else ever could. I honestly believe that serving God is the most effective method we can employ to aid in coping with grief. I do not serve God for the therapeutic value, I serve

Him because I love Him. However, I learned a long time ago that you cannot out-give God. The Bible says in Luke 6:38, "Give, and it shall be given unto you; good measure, pressed down, and shaken together, and running over, shall men give into your bosom. For with the same measure that ye mete withal it shall be measured to you again." Give your life to serve God and I guarantee He will bless you abundantly. If you were involved in the Lord's work before your loss, stay involved. If you previously were not involved in His work, find a way to get involved. Perhaps you might join the choir in your church. Offer to be a greeter at the door. Mow the lawn around the church house. Hand out gospel tracts and tell folks how to get to Heaven. Surely you can find some way to serve God.

> *Serving God is the most effective method we can employ to aid in coping with grief.*

In this brand-new chapter of your life, you may see opportunities to serve the Lord that have been enhanced or may not have even existed before. Have you ever stopped to think that having recently lost a loved one gives you an edge in soul winning? The morning Debbie left for Heaven, I had the privilege of leading the Hospice nurse to the Lord! That was a sad but thrilling morning for me! I am so glad I chose to serve God in the midst of my grief! Either way, Debbie was gone, but I could have missed a blessing. Other times, while talking to folks about the Lord, I have stressed the importance of knowing for sure that their eternal destiny was Heaven.

I would tell them that my wife recently left for her heavenly home. Often that would get their attention and they would allow me to show them from the Bible how they too could have that assurance. Several have gotten saved! The Bible says in I Corinthians 15:58, "Therefore, my beloved brethren, be ye stedfast, unmoveable, always abounding in the work of the Lord, forasmuch as ye know that your labour is not in vain in the Lord."

I wonder what Debbie would have to say if she could give me a call. What advice would your departed loved one offer? I am quite sure they would tell of the splendors of Heaven and of conversations with other friends and loved ones who have gone before us. Beyond the chitchat, the most important thing on their minds, I believe, would be to challenge us to use our remaining time for the glory of God. After the rich man in Hell realized that he could not have a drop of water to cool his tongue, he immediately began to think of others who needed to hear the gospel. If a lost man in Hell has a burden for souls, do you not think that a child of God in Heaven would share that same concern? Surely, they would hope that we would share Christ with the rest of the family who may not know the Lord. They would say, "Time is of the essence, tell them before it's too late." I have no doubt, Debbie would tell me, "Rod, there is nothing more important than serving God—Don't stop now!" I believe, more than ever, especially considering their heavenly perspective, every one of our loved ones who have gone before us would plead with us to get busy for God. Yes, I grieve. Yes, I cry, but I am not going to stop serving God.

CHAPTER 8

God Offers Comfort to the Mourner

In Matthew 5:4, Jesus makes an amazing statement: "Blessed are they that mourn: for they shall be comforted." Earlier we took note of the fact that Job mourned his loss. When the Lord takes a loved one home we are going to mourn. Have you ever considered the thought that perhaps God empathizes with us when a loved one dies? God's only begotten Son died a cruel death on a cross for sins He did not even commit. God very willingly allowed Jesus to suffer and die, because that was the only way you and I and our loved ones could ever get to Heaven. God loves us that much! Do you not think it ripped His heart out when Jesus suffered such a horrible death? I am convinced that our Heavenly Father understands the hurt and pain we feel. God in His love made a way for you and me to receive comfort when we mourn the death of a loved one. The Apostle Paul elaborates on this in II Corinthians 1:3-7. In these verses, Paul shows us that we should allow God and our Christian friends to comfort us.

> *Our God is the God of all comfort!*

"Blessed be God, even the Father of our Lord Jesus Christ, the Father of mercies, and the God of all comfort;

Who comforteth us in all our tribulation, that we may be able to comfort them which are in any trouble, by the comfort wherewith we ourselves are comforted of God.

For as the sufferings of Christ abound in us, so our consolation also aboundeth by Christ.

And whether we be afflicted, it is for your consolation and salvation, which is effectual in the enduring of the same sufferings which we also suffer: or whether we be comforted, it is for your consolation and salvation.

And our hope of you is stedfast, knowing, that as ye are partakers of the sufferings, so shall ye be also of the consolation." (II Corinthians 1:3-7)

Our God is the God of all comfort! (Verse 3) There are so many perks for having a relationship with the God of Heaven! When we are in need of comfort, the best thing we can do is get close to the Lord. Do your best to meet with Him in His house every time the doors are open. Spend time with Him in prayer. Talk to God, tell Him how much you miss your loved one, thank Him for all the special memories. Read a portion of Scripture every day; often this is the way God will speak back to you after you have talked to Him. At times, He will draw our attention to a particular verse or thought that we may have overlooked in the past. In that passage, we then find the help, comfort, or answer we were looking for! In James 4:8, the Bible says, "Draw nigh to God, and he will draw nigh to you." Friend, stay close to God, especially during your time of grief. While you are close to God, you will naturally find yourself close to others who are close to Him as well. Many of our Christian friends have also had to say goodbye to a parent, a spouse, a child, or close friend. At that time, they received comfort from God and their Christian friends. They know what you are going through; they have been there. Let them encourage you. This is one of the ways the God of all comfort helps to meet your need in these difficult times. Look at verse 4 one more time.

> *"Who comforteth us in all our tribulation, that we may be able to comfort them which are in any trouble, by the comfort wherewith we ourselves are comforted of God."*
> (II Corinthians 1:4)

Do you see what God is trying to do for us? Others who were comforted by God in the past, are now reaching out to us with the comfort that they received from Him in their time of grief. By the way, remember, you and I will have a responsibility to do the same. I think that might be a great example of paying it forward. God's plan is always the best plan. In this case, it's a family plan. The Heavenly Father does not single handedly bring you comfort, rather, He directs your Christian siblings to work with Him, ensuring that you sense God's loving touch from every angle. Your grieving will be much harder and last much longer if you try to go it alone. I am humbled by the way God's children have been such a help to me since Debbie's homegoing. Cards, letters, phone calls, monetary gifts, hugs—I really appreciate the hugs. Folks have demonstrated to me

> *Your grieving will be much harder and last much longer if you try to go it alone.*

that they really care. When friends ask how you are doing, they care about you and want to help. There is no reason to be embarrassed by giving a truthful answer. An out-of-state pastor friend who had also lost his wife just a few years ago called me a short time after Debbie had passed and asked how I was doing. I told him, "Well... the default answer is, I'm doing alright." He replied, "Brother Rod, we used to call that a lie." My friend helped me that day.

The Apostle Paul assured us that though we all will suffer; we all will be consoled by God.

> "*And our hope of you is stedfast, knowing, that as ye are partakers of the sufferings, so shall ye be also of the consolation.*" (II Corinthians 1:7)

Let the God of all comfort meet your need like no one else can. The psalmist implies in Psalm 27:13,14 that he would not have made it through a particularly hard time in his life had he not believed in God's goodness.

> "*I had fainted, unless I had believed to see the goodness of the LORD in the land of the living.*
>
> *Wait on the LORD: be of good courage, and he shall strengthen thine heart: wait, I say, on the LORD.*" (Psalm 27:3,4)

I too might not have made it had I not believed that God was being good to me in the land of the living. We are confident that our loved one sees the goodness of the Lord in Heaven; but what about us? He is being good to her, but what about me? We may feel alone, possibly even forsaken by God. Satan may put those thoughts our minds, but we know deep down in our hearts that God is not like that. My friend, your heavenly Father loves you beyond measure. We can have confidence that God is just as good to us who are left here in the land of the living as He is to our loved ones who have died and are with Him in Glory. Some folks question God's love for them; they refuse to wait for His comfort and thereby miss the amazing touch of God as He attempts to strengthen their heart. Accept David's challenge to wait on the Lord.

> *Some folks refuse to wait for His comfort and thereby miss the amazing touch of God.*

Remember, back in the introduction, we saw that God's perspective on the death of a Christian was stated in Psalm 116:15; "Precious in the sight of the LORD is the death of his saints." If we handle things Scripturally, although it is not easy, and we will certainly mourn, it can be a precious time for us as well.

CHAPTER 9

Verify Your Reservation for Heaven

The greatest comfort available to you and me is the assurance that we will see our loved ones in Heaven. The fact that you are even reading this book tells me that you believe your loved one is a child of God. Without a doubt, all of God's children go to Heaven. The next step would be to verify that you too, are a child of God. Some might say, "I thought all people are God's children." It is understandable how folks could arrive at that conclusion. It is true that all of mankind are part of His creation; however, the Bible teaches us that only those born into His family are His children. In the gospel of John chapter 3, Jesus is explaining this to a man named Nicodemus.

> *"Jesus answered and said unto him, Verily, verily, I say unto thee, Except a man be born again, he cannot see the kingdom of God."* (John 3:3)

Jesus goes on to explain that obviously we all have a physical birth, but that we also need a spiritual birth to get to Heaven. Hence the terms, "born again" or "new birth." Later in the same chapter, Jesus makes a statement that most people are familiar with.

> *"For God so loved the world, that he gave his only begotten Son, that whosoever believeth in him should not perish, but have everlasting life."* (John 3:16)

Believing in Jesus, the Son of God, is the only way to Heaven. Those who do not have everlasting life in Heaven, "perish" in Hell. The last verse in John chapter 3 also emphasizes this.

> *"He that believeth on the Son hath everlasting life: and he that believeth not the Son shall not see life; but the wrath of God abideth on him."* (John 3:36)

In the book of Romans, God laid out in detail how to be born again. First, God points out the fact that we are all sinners.

> *"For all have sinned, and come short of the glory of God;"* (Romans 3:23)

Next, He wants us to be aware of the penalty for being a sinner. Romans 6:23 is a tremendous verse because it first gives the penalty for our sin but then goes on to tell of the pardon that God has provided!

> *"For the wages of sin is death; but the gift of God is eternal life through Jesus Christ our Lord."* (Romans 6:23)

The wages of sin is death or eternal damnation in a literal place called Hell. (The Bible also refers to Hell as the second death.) We deserve to go to Hell—we have earned it. Eternal life on the other hand cannot be earned—it is a gift! Jesus, by shedding his perfect sinless blood on the cross, paid the penalty for our sin. My friend, apart from Jesus Christ, we have no hope. The following three verses explain that in our weak and sinful condition, it would be highly unlikely that anyone would die for us. In reality, Jesus was the only one who *could* die for us; any other man's death would be to no avail.

> *"For when we were yet without strength, in due time Christ died for the ungodly.*
>
> *For scarcely for a righteous man will one die: yet peradventure for a good man some would even dare to die.*
>
> *But God commendeth his love toward us, in that, while we were yet sinners, Christ died for us".* (Romans 5:6-8)

Jesus Christ, our only Hope, did die in our place. He then rose from the dead three days later just like He said He would. Today, He offers the only acceptable payment for our sin, in the form of a gift. The Bible tells us how to receive the gift of eternal life and be saved or born again:

> *"That if thou shalt confess with thy mouth the Lord Jesus, and shalt believe in thine heart that God hath raised him from the dead, thou shalt be saved.*
>
> *For with the heart man believeth unto righteousness; and with the mouth confession is made unto salvation."* (Romans 10:9,10)

Friend, you must recognize the fact that you are a sinner who deserves to spend an eternity in Hell. Then believe that Jesus loved you so much, that He died for you to pay for your sins. Believe that He did not stay in the grave but rose again the third day. Be truly sorry for your sin; you have offended the Almighty God. Finally, ask Jesus to forgive you, and then ask Him for the gift of eternal life.

> *"For whosoever shall call upon the name of the Lord shall be saved."* (Romans 10:13)

To make your reservation in Heaven you could, right where you are, and in your own words, call upon the Lord.

- Admit to Him that you are a sinner and deserve to spend eternity in Hell.
- Tell God how sorry you are for all the sins you have committed.
- Let Him know that you believe that His Son, Jesus, died on the cross to pay for your sins, and that He is the only Way to Heaven.
- Finally, ask Him to save you and take you to Heaven when you die.
- Remember to thank Him!

Rest assured God will hear your prayer and He will do for you exactly what He promised in the verse quoted above. (Romans 10:13)

If you just asked Jesus to save you, I am very happy for you. You and your loved one will be reunited and then spend an eternity together in Heaven! Debbie was a soul winner. She wanted everyone to have peace in their hearts like she did. She gave out gospel tracts and when she had opportunity, she would tell people how to get to Heaven. I believe that Debbie is rejoicing with the angels today over the fact that you are now a child of God!

I want to challenge you to let your friends and family know of your decision to trust Jesus Christ as your Saviour. When the Lord calls you home it will be a comfort to them if they know you are in Heaven.

A Song from Debbie

*D*ebbie had a special gift from God to write music. The following are the lyrics to a song that Debbie wrote back in 2010. It is sure to bless your heart. I wish that I could somehow sing it for you—it is absolutely beautiful. We hope to eventually be able to put the music on paper so others can use it. Two additional songs that will help comfort a grieving heart, *God Is Already There* and *There's A Land* can both be found in Debbie's "Songs for My King" series.

I Have Just Begun To Live

Verse 1

When we face the loss of someone very dear,
Though we try to be strong, we still shed many tears;
But if our loved one knew the Lord before departure day,
And if he could send a message, this is what he'd say:

Chorus

"I have just begun to live—at last these eyes can truly see;
From sin and shame unshackled, from death forever free.
I can look upon the face of our loving Lamb of Grace;
No need for tears of grief—I have joy beyond belief—
And I have just begun to live."

Verse 2

One day you may hear that I am dead and gone;
Let me tell you now, my friend, I still live on!
I've only changed my residence to Heaven's mansion fair—
And if you listen closely, I'll call from over there:

Chorus

"I have just begun to live—at last these eyes can truly see;
From sin and shame unshackled, from death forever free.
I can look upon the face of our loving Lamb of Grace;
No need for tears of grief—I have joy beyond belief—
And I have just begun,
Thanks to God's dear Son,
I have just begun to live."

Music by Debbie Black

Songs for My King Volume 1

But God
God Is Already There
The Blood
So Near to the King
Unto Us A Child Is Born

Songs for My King Volume 2

Cradled In Mercy
Missions: The Heartbeat of God
Our Wedding Day
Paid In Full
The Choice
There's A Land

Songs for My King Volume 3

A Time To Remember
How Many More Will Die Before We Go?
I Want to Make a Difference
My Hiding Place
No Turning Back

Patriotic songs: *(individually bound)*

American Legacy
Pray for America
I'll Not Forget

Music available at sermonandsong.org

Debbie Black Memorial Church Pianist Scholarship Fund

During our nearly 20 years in evangelism Debbie and I saw an increasing lack of church pianists. While some churches may have several capable piano players, an alarming number have none. Every church needs a pianist. If you or someone you know could benefit from this scholarship fund you may find more information at sermonandsong.org. Perhaps you too have a heart to help train church pianists, consider making a donation or possibly supporting this fund on a monthly basis.

An Additional Resource

Hope for Hurting Hearts
<u>A Journey of Healing</u> by Dr. Don Woodard

Note: Debbie Black Invested a considerable amount of time assisting Dr. Woodard with this project several years ago. This was during a time in her life that she was experiencing chronic nerve pain caused by the shingles. For approximately two years, Debbie could not sit down without experiencing extreme pain. She would often stand in the back of the auditorium during the entire Sunday school hour and the whole church service as well. Many times, the pastor of the church I was preaching in, would take us out to eat after the service—she would stand at the table throughout the whole meal. After the manuscript was completed, Debbie told me that the content really helped her in dealing with her situation. This book will be a help to you, whether you find yourself grieving or possibly experiencing some other particularly difficult storm or time of tribulation in your life. After Debbie's homegoing, other than my daily Bible reading, this was the first book I read.

Available at:

drdonwoodard.com
LightKeeper Publications
PO Box 490, Troutville, VA 24175
540-354-8573